better together*

*This book is best read together, grownup and kid.

a kids
book
about™

a kids book about

DISABILITIES

by Kristine Napper

a kids book about™

A Kids Book About books are exclusively available online
on the A Kids Book About website.

To share your stories, ask questions, or inquire about bulk
purchases (schools, libraries, and nonprofits), please use
the following email address:

hello@akidsbookabout.com

www.akidsbookabout.com

ISBN: 9781951253257

To my parents, Karen and Ken, who have supported me through every dream, every whim, and every obstacle.

Intro

Kids ask all kinds of questions about my wheelchair, but grownups' most frequent question is: "How should we talk about disability with kids?" They want the kids in their lives to be curious and informed as well as inclusive and accepting. These are great goals! But grownups are also afraid of saying the wrong thing or accidentally offending someone.

This book can be read with kids who have disabilities, know people with disabilities, or will meet disabled people out in the world—in other words, it's for everyone!

I can't answer all of your questions and I can't speak on behalf of all disabled people, but I can tell you about my own experience and help you start some conversations. It's OK if you don't know the answer to every question that might come up. Just talking about disability helps erase stigma.

So let's talk!

Hi, my name is Kristine.

If you could see me right now,

You'd see...

brown hair with a **little purple** in the front,
some dangly earrings,
a cozy sweater,
and a pretty purple wheelchair
(I call her Lydia).

That's right, I have a **disability**.

I was born with **SMA**,
which stands for
Spinal **M**uscular **A**trophy.

It affects my whole body,
making my muscles weaker.

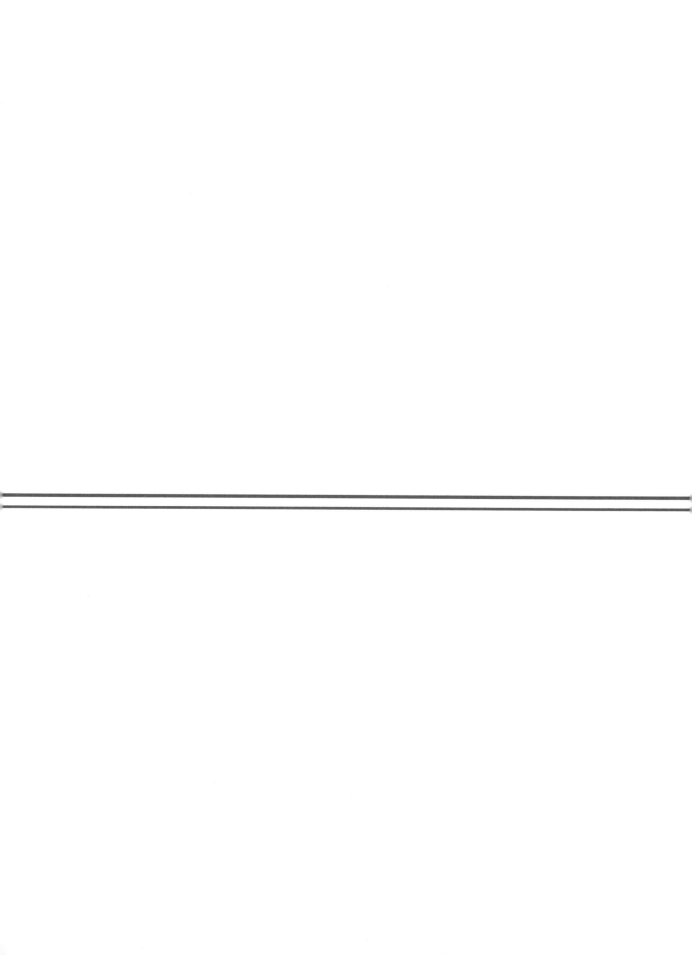

While I can't stand up and walk around, *my chair goes really fast!*

Sometimes when people see me and my chair...

they get uncomfortable,
they don't know what to say,
they talk to me like I'm stupid,
they ask really personal questions,
they feel sorry for me,
and sometimes they just
stare at me with a sad face.

Would you like people greeting you this way?

Not just once or twice, but *all the time?*

Probably not.

When they do this, it's not because...

of my brown eyes,

or short hair,

and it's not because they're having a bad day.

It's because I have a disability.

Having a disability means you can't do something the way most people do, so you find a **different** way.

And there are even different kinds of disabilities:

physical, intellectual, emotional, learning, behavioral, and so many more.

I've learned a lot from living with a disability, so I'd like to share some things with you.

The **first** thing to know

about people with disabilities is ▪ ▪ ▪ ▪ ▪ ▪

we are normal.

Yup, that's right.

We're not scary monsters, space aliens, or sad stories.

Normal people
come in all different
shapes,
sizes,
& colors.

Being normal means being different.

Having a disability is one of the MANY ways to be normal.

If you understand that disabled people are normal, then you'll have no problem with everything else we're going to talk about.

And guess what.......

you're usually really good at this!

Sorry grownups, you're usually not.

Kids are good at being curious and respectful, including and not excluding.

Grownups are usually just afraid they'll say or do the wrong thing.

So if my disability is normal,
how do you think I like to be treated?

NOR

MAL

■■■■■■■■□□ That's right—treat me normally!

You might wonder whether it's OK to help me. The answer is, sometimes.

There are lots of things I can do on my own,
but some things I need help with.

I might ask for your help opening a door,
reaching something off the floor,
or taking the cap off a marker.

If you think I might need help, it's OK to ask. I'll either say:

"Yes, please!" or *"No, thank you."*

But if I say no, please listen,
because forced help really isn't helpful.

Another thing—I don't like being stared at. It's just not polite.

If you have a question about me, my chair, or my disability, it's OK to ask.

Most of the time, it's totally OK!

But some questions aren't nice.
Some are kinda mean.
Questions like ■■■■■■■■■■■■■■■■■■■■■

"What's wrong with you?"

"Tell me how you use the bathroom?"

"What happened to you?"

"Can you have babies?"

Try to avoid questions that will make
the other person feel bad or embarrassed.

So what do you talk about with
a person who has a disability?

HING!

Say,
"*Hi, how are you?*
How's your day going?"
Ask about what movies I like,
where I grew up,
or my favorite ice cream flavor.
(It's cookie dough)

I love talking about my disability, but it's not the ONLY thing I want to talk about.

One last thing I want you to know,
is I am not broken.

I don't need to be fixed.

In fact, my disability helps me be
a wiser, kinder, stronger person.

But, there is something really important
that needs to change.......

THE W

ORLD

There are places I can't go,
because nobody built a ramp or elevator.

I almost never see people with disabilities like mine on TV, in movies, or in books.

I have a job that I love (I'm a teacher).

But I know lots of disabled people who can't get jobs even though they *want* to work.

So,
try to notice
when people with disabilities are

left out,
excluded,
or...

The world needs to be more accessible.

People need to be more inclusive.

Disabled people belong everywhere.

That's what normal looks like.

Outro

I hope this book answered some questions. More importantly, I hope it inspires new questions! I didn't explain every big word or big idea introduced in this book—a book that big wouldn't fit on a shelf—but I hope you'll take the opportunity to dig deeper into anything that sparked curiosity. Kids and grownups can learn together about different disabilities, interesting people who have disabilities, and how to make the world more accessible for disabled people.

As the kids in your life become comfortable with the different ways people navigate the world, you might be surprised by their brilliant ideas for improving accessibility. Their open minds and hearts might even help change the world. Thank you for starting the conversations!

find more kids books about

bullying, creativity, racism, divorce, empathy, shame, adventure, belonging, failure, money, and anxiety.

akidsbookabout.com

share
your read*

*Tell someboady, post a photo, or give this book away to share what you care about.

@akidsbookabout